Ten Principles

Happy Marriage

KT-214-323

Titles in the Christian Counselling Series

Ten Principles for a Happy Marriage

Selwyn Hughes

Marshalls

Marshalls Paperbacks
Marshall Morgan & Scott
3 Beggarwood Lane, Basingstoke, Hants, UK

Copyright © Selwyn Hughes 1982
First published by Marshall Morgan & Scott 1982

Reprinted
Impression number
84 85 86 87: 8 7 6 5 4 3

ISBN 0 551 00947 0

Printed in Great Britain by
Richard Clay (The Chaucer Press) Ltd,
Bungay, Suffolk

Contents

Preface

The books in the *Christian Counselling Series* are written with two main groups of people in mind. The first group are those who facing a personal problem look for something concise and readable that speaks to their need. The second group are ministers and counsellors who wish to place in the hands of people seeking help something that will supplement their own individual counselling efforts.

The authors, writing from their own personal encounters with people who have faced the problems listed in this series, do so with a good deal of confidence. They claim that when the principles outlined in these books have been followed they have contributed in a positive manner to helping people resolve their difficulties. The content is firmly based on Scripture, but the authors in their writing seek to apply Biblical principles in such a way that helps readers, not only to know what they should do but how to do it.

Introduction

Beryl came into the counselling room with tears running down her face: 'This is the sixth year running' she said 'that my husband has forgotten our wedding anniversary. The way he treats me shows exactly what he thinks of me deep down in his heart.' She went on to say that in recent months the joy of marriage had begun to fade and she wondered if this was the time when they should both share their problems with a marriage guidance counsellor.

Within a few days I set up several appointments which were designed to overhaul their marriage. We discovered, as we so often do in counselling, that there are a number of well-defined factors which go to make the difference between a happy marriage and an unhappy one. Helping Christians resolve their differences in marriage has been one of my main concerns ever since I became a minister, now over thirty years ago, and during this time I have been able to log certain facts about what makes a marriage happy – and what doesn't. Some of these facts I shared with Beryl and her husband and after facing several personal challenges it was not long before they began to experience marital happiness once again. In these pages I intend to share with you some of the things I present to those who come to me and ask for counselling in connection with their marital problems.

God's purpose in marriage

Since God created man and woman for each other it follows that the best advice on marriage will be found in God's manual of instruction – the Bible. God not only made the product, man and woman, but gave a handbook of instruction to go along with it, the Scriptures. The Bible is the best textbook on the subject of interpersonal relationships in existence and it contains the basic principles of how to make a marriage work.

Let's see, firstly, what the Bible has to say about the creation of man and woman: 'And the Lord God said, It is not good that the man should be alone: I will make him an help-meet for him . . . and Adam said, This is now bone of my bones, and flesh of my flesh: she shall be called Woman, because she was taken out of Man. Therefore shall a man leave his father and mother, and shall cleave unto his wife: and they shall be one flesh' (Genesis 2.18, 23, 24). When God joined a man and a woman together in what can be described as *The World's First Wedding*, Adam immediately recognised Eve as being an indispensable part of his happiness. The Revised Standard Version puts it like this: 'Then the man said, This *at last* is bone of my bones' (Genesis 2.33). Some commentators feel that the expression *at last* suggests that as soon as Adam saw the woman whom God had created for him he sensed that in her was the answer to the inner longings of his personality. Generally speaking there is a need in man which only a woman can meet (and vice versa) and allowing for the fact that God calls some people to celibacy, God's usual purpose is for a man and a woman to be joined together in matrimony for the procreation of mankind and the mutual affection one with the other.

The institution of marriage is in trouble

In his book *Future Shock* Alvin Toffler predicts that in the foreseeable future the institution of marriage will be subjected to some several sociological pressures that will greatly affect the family unit as we now know it. He claims that there will be a general acceptance of temporary marriages and an apprenticeship period of five years, at the end of which married couples will have an option to renew their marriage licence or revoke it – according to the desire of the couple concerned. Any children resulting from such a marriage will be fostered by government trained foster parents whose professional task it will be to care for the children of dissolved marriages.

At this very moment we are passing through a period when there is an increasing public acceptance of broken or unhappy marriages and a decreasing sense of its stigma. Dr James Hemming writing in 'Marriage Guidance', the official organ of the Marriage Guidance Council, predicts 'Engagement rings are doomed, weddings will be rituals of the past. Couples will wed only after they have lived together.' The Associated Press commenting on Hemming's statements, said, 'If Dr Hemming is right the word "marriage" itself could become obsolete in the foreseeable future.'

Even in Church circles there are deep and disturbing signs that the pressures through which society is passing are beginning to have an effect upon Christian marriages. Easier divorce is becoming for many an escape route from their problems, but divorce is seldom a solution. God's highest purpose for all married couples is for them to establish a happy and meaningful family life. Society may have few clear answers to the problems of living together happily as man and wife, but the Scripture has a wealth of material to offer on the subject. Based on my study of the Scriptures, and my experience in working with hundreds of couples over several decades, I offer the following as a basis for a happy and successful marriage.

1

Correct any faulty standards developed during your courtship period

If a couple engage in pre-marital sex they commit what the Bible calls 'fornication' (1 Cor. 5.1). This is a sin in God's sight and a definite violation of His design for human relationships. However modern day society might look at it God looks upon it as sin and until it is brought to God, confessed and dealt with in the right way, it can bring about an undermining of a marriage. I know this might sound strange and unnecessary to some Christians as they believe that although they may have engaged in pre-marital sex, now they are married the subject can happily be forgotten.

But it's not quite as easy as that! Any violation of God's commandments can only be effectively dealt with by an act of true repentance where those who have violated God's order take the necessary steps to clear up the transgression. This means that the couple should first ask God's forgiveness and then seek forgiveness from each other.

In my counselling experience I have been amazed at the number of times that problems between couples have been rooted in faulty courtship standards. I remember one couple who shared with me, over many hours, a long list of their problems. One by one they were dissolved, but in a few weeks they were back again in the counselling room and said that the tension and hostility between them was now even worse. It was at this point that I decided to ask them about their relationship during their courtship period. They then became extremely diffident and uncommunicative. I explained my reasons for wanting to know, and eventually they shared with me that they had engaged frequently in pre-marital sex. I explained that this was a violation of God's order, to which they both agreed and it was at this point that they jointly remarked 'But now we are married isn't that in the past?' I pointed them to the church at Ephesus as recorded in Revelation 2.1–7. This church had lapsed in its love for Christ and had turned away from what the Bible calls 'it's first love'. Christ stands before the church and confronts them with the reality of their behaviour and calls upon them to repent. Notice Christ did not say 'If you get your first love back then we can forget everything that has gone on before'. No, He was too wise a counsellor to do that, for violated Biblical principles do not disappear of their own accord; they must be dealt with properly by a clear act of repentance. So His word is clear and insistent: 'Remember from whence thou art fallen and *repent*.'

I then encouraged the couple to ask God's forgiveness for this violation, and then to ask forgiveness of each other. This they did in my presence.

Immediately they had prayed and then turned to each other and said 'I'm sorry for my involvement in breaking God's standards in our courtship days – will you forgive me?' the sense of release that came into their lives was remarkable. The man said, 'I can see now that all through our marriage I have carried this as a cloud of guilt which I thought had been cancelled when we got married. Now, however, I realise by the very nature of the situation that it could not be dissolved of its own accord. It needed firm action. Thank you for helping us see it.'

The woman at this stage said very little but when I spoke to her some weeks later she said something to me that was quite revealing, although I have heard it hundreds of times since. It was this: 'Before we came for counselling I used to say to myself "I wonder would . . . have married me if I hadn't allowed him to have sex with me?" That doubt was always there, lying in my mind, but when he asked my forgiveness over the matter the doubt disappeared. I know now that our marriage is on a firm and strong foundation.'

Since that time I have always encouraged couples who have engaged in pre-marital sex to firmly deal with the matter, asking God's forgiveness and then the forgiveness of each other. An unresolved conflict such as this can lie at the base of a marriage and undermine its foundations. Guilt remains when violated spiritual principles are not corrected. Such an important issue should not be left to chance, but dealt with by a genuine act of confession and repentance.

2

Maintain the proper
Scriptural roles

One of the greatest areas of concern in many of today's marriages centres around the roles of husband and wife. The traditional role of the woman keeping house is unfulfilling to many wives in this modern generation and the trend toward women working outside the home has brought about new attitudes to the matter of family roles.

Professor Howard G. Hendricks in his book 'Heaven Help the Home' says that 'roles always determine relationships.' In other words if you don't have a clear understanding of the role God wants you to play in your marriage, then it will soon undermine your relationships. An understanding of the roles which God has given a man and a woman to fulfil in their marriage is of the utmost importance to the preservation and happiness of a marriage. There are some, I know, who will raise their eyebrows and say 'Roles? What need do we have of roles? This is the twentieth century – with equal rights; no sex discrimination', and so on. Well, admittedly, the idea of roles in marriage is almost lost in the pollution of this mixed-up age through which we are passing, but despite the blurring of the issue by modern men and women the Scripture quite clearly emphasises its continuing importance.

In the book of Ephesians, chapter 5, Paul interprets God's mind on the issue of family roles and relationships. The husband is described as 'the head of the wife' (v.23) implying authority and headship. This does not mean, however, that a man is to be a dictator who bullies his wife into submission by such commands as 'Get me my bedroom slippers', 'make sure my dinner is on the table when I get home', or 'obey me in everything I say'. He is to wield this authority by love: 'Husbands love your wives as Christ loved the Church' (v.25). And how does Christ love the Church? Not by bullying it into submission, or by issuing stern commands. But by gently, compassionately and tenderly wooing the Church to His standards and principles. A wrong concept of headship will produce the way of enforced submission in which there is no true joy or peace. To see what true headship means we must see it as expressed in the Godhead. Paul, in 1 Corinthians 11.3, says 'the head of Christ is God.' This does not mean that God is greater than Christ, for we know from other Scriptural references that Christ and God are co-equal and co-eternal (John 1.1, John 10.30). It is a *voluntary* subordination – Christ puts Himself under the Father's authority for the purposes of redemption. God does not force Christ into submission by an act of domination, but by love. God's love for the Son produces the true loving submission of Jesus.

If a man sees Jesus, his head, as a *dominating* ruler then he will become dominating in his own relationship with his wife and family. If also his spirit is strong and unbroken he will reach out for such Scriptures as 'wives submit to your husbands' and move in the spirit of a ruler to enforce it for his own benefit. When a man seeks headship for himself and submission for his wife he is only seeking to set up his own kingdom – not God's. It may even be possible that his primary objective is to overthrow *her* kingdom in order to set up his own – and this only produces war. A woman will find it difficult to be truly one in spirit, soul and body with a husband who is always dominating her.

Whenever I counsel a couple who say that their marriage lacks love I look for the deficiency first in the husband. God has designed a man to be a love-initiator and a woman to be a love receiver. This is a generalisation, of course, because a woman is required to love too, but basically the main ministry of a man in marriage is to love his wife so that in the depth of her personality she experiences the inner glow of being loved. When a man functions in this way he is fulfilling his Scriptural role of being a loving leader.

The wife, on the other hand, is required by God to be *joyfully submissive*: 'Wives submit yourselves unto your own husbands as unto the Lord.' I have included the word 'joyfully' here because some women see 'submission' as threatening. One woman once said to me, as she gritted her teeth, 'Well, if God wants me to be submissive to my husband then

I will be submissive.' She missed the point of the Scripture's exhortation, for if submission is not given joyously it will hinder the marriage relationship, rather than help. Listen once again to what the Scripture says: 'Wives be submissive to your own husbands *as unto the Lord*.' If a woman has difficulty in submitting to her husband her main problem is not between her and her husband but between her and the Lord. She fails to see that this requirement is not a device of husbands to get their wives to submit to them but a commandment of the Lord.

I recognise, of course, that some women find it extremely difficult to be submissive, because from the early days of their marriage they were obliged, by reason of their husband's weakness or inadequacy, to take the initiative and play a leadership role. But this is no reason for maintaining a role that is not provided for in Scripture. A woman is designed to *lean* and not to lead in a marriage, and if she finds herself leading then she ought to stand back and take a look at herself in the light of the Scripture's commands. Many men are quite content to let their wives lead, and in this case a woman must *gently* pull back from a leadership role, letting the responsibility fall *gradually* upon her husband so that he begins to function in the way God designed him.

Some women, on the other hand, take this issue of submission too far and become overly submissive. They obey everything their husbands tell them to do without equivocation. If a husband gives his wife a command that is clearly unscriptural then she is free to disobey. But in disobeying she must make it clear that her intention is to obey as far as possible in her marriage, but that when she is asked to violate a Biblical principle then her loyalty to Christ must take priority. What God wants to develop in a woman is a *spirit* of obedience. When a man recognises in his wife a sincere longing to follow out the role God has designed for her, that of being joyfully submissive, it will in most cases affect his inner attitudes and, in turn, help him to become the man God wants him to be. After talking to hundreds of men and women in marriage guidance sessions, I have come to the conclusion that a man's greatest fear is that he might be dominated by his wife, and a woman's greatest fear is that she will be treated as an object and not as a person. When a man and woman follow God's roles for their marriage those fears will never arise.

3

Keep the lines of communication continually open

Love in a marriage sometimes fades, not so much from angry battles, sexual frustration, financial problems, or in-law difficulties, but because it exhausts itself trying to scale the wall of a communication failure. Those who take time to learn the principles of effective communication will discover, as a result, a new dimension in their marriage. Most marriage counsellors list communication difficulties as a major cause of marital difficulty, but it is not only a difficulty in itself – it often shows up as a symptom of wider, more disturbing problems.

A recent research amongst marriage guidance counsellors where several hundred happily married couples were compared with the same number of unhappily married couples, came up with the following conclusions. The happily married couples (1) talked more to each other, (2) conveyed the feeling that they understood what was being said to them, (3) had a wider range of conversational subjects, (4) showed sensitivity to the feelings of the other partner, and (5) sought to keep communication channels open. As a counsellor I'm tired of hearing people say they want to get a divorce because they can't work out their problems. In most cases the reason their marriage is in difficulty is because they are either too proud or too lazy to work on their problems. Divorce is not the only way out that so many people think.

There is no doubt that the heart of a marriage is its communication system. Communication has been defined as 'the process in which two people share both verbally and non-verbally in such a way that their message is accepted and understood.' Communication in marriage consists of three components: talking, listening and understanding. Let's take them one by one. *Talking:* No marriage can grow or develop unless the partners take time to talk to each other. If a married couple are extremely busy with a growing family, or business demands, they should allocate certain times of the day for the purpose of just talking together. These times should be seen as creative opportunities to share their thoughts and feelings with each other, for it is only in the sharing of thoughts and feelings that mutual respect, trust and love can flourish.

Talking involves the use of words, and words, as the Scriptures tell us, are immensely powerful: 'Death and life are in the power of the tongue' (Proverbs 18.21) They can blister or they can bless: they can wound or they can heal. So pay attention to the words you speak. When God spoke in Genesis 1 He created a world – a world of order and a world of beauty. When you speak you too create a world – a world of cosmos or a world of chaos. So choose your words carefully, remembering that harsh words hurt, gentle words heal.

The second component of communication is *listening*. Many marriage partners concentrate so much on getting their point across in a conversation that they fail to pay attention to cultivating the art of listening. An invaluable device in building good communication techniques, particularly when you are discussing a relationship problem, is to practice listening to your partner without interrupting. Then re-phrase your partner's statement and reflect it back. Your partner then has the opportunity to confirm that what you have heard is precisely what he intended to convey, or if not, a correction can then be made. Try it sometime. It takes discipline, but it can be a valuable tool in building good relationships.

Listening has been defined as 'not thinking about what you are going to say when the other person has finished speaking'. If you focus on what you are going to say rather than on what the other person is saying, you might miss the real import of the communication. Listening is concentrating so much on what the other person is saying that you become more conscious of them than you are of yourself.

The third component of communication is *understanding*. Try to understand not just what your partner is saying but *why* he or she is saying it. This does not mean that you have to play the game of 'amateur psychologist' but seek to understand the context in which your partner makes decisions, or arrives at conclusions. For example, a woman I know who used to get extremely irritated with her husband whenever he opposed her over buying even an inexpensive item for the home, was introduced to the concept of trying to understand why her husband acted in this way. One day she said to him 'Darling, help me understand the difficulty you have in agreeing to buy small and necessary things for the home.' The husband was taken aback for a moment but, with a little gentle and genuinely loving persuasion, he began to share with her that having been brought up in an atmosphere of frugality he found it difficult to spend money on anything unless it was an absolute and urgent necessity. His wife responded to this by saying she could understand why and how he felt that way, bearing in mind the circumstances under which he had been brought up, and that she would do her utmost in future to keep purchases to a minimum. Immediately the man felt his wife understood him he began to change. Within weeks his attitude was completely different and, although he still had negative feelings about making purchases, in the atmosphere of loving acceptance given to him by his wife he surmounted his problem and, to a great extent overcame a life-long difficulty. It is absolutely amazing how people change when they know they are understood.

4

Concentrate on meeting your partner's basic need

We saw earlier that in Genesis 2.18 God said that it was not good for the man to be alone. Malachi speaks of a wife as a companion by covenant (Malachi 2.14) and so marriage can be considered as a relationship in which God designs that each person be an instrument to meet the needs of the other. A Christian psychologist, by the name of Lawrence Crabb, after studying the subject of marriage for many years in a clinical context, says that a husband's most basic need is *significance* (adequacy, respect, admiration) while a wife's most central need appears to be that of *security* (love, acceptance, sensitive and thoughtful caring). God's plan is for husbands to minister to their wife's need for security and for wives to minister to their husband's need for significance.

Whilst this is God's plan for marriage, the truth is that, in practice, most marriages fail to function in this way. Husbands view marriage as an opportunity to feel significant through their wives. And wives, in turn, think of their husbands, not as someone to whom they can minister, but rather as a source of their own security. Instead of focussing on being a *giver* each partner focusses on being a getter: each partner looks to the other to meet his or her needs. In fact, the key problem behind most marital difficulties lies right here – husbands depend on their wives to make them feel significant and wives depend on their husbands to make them feel secure. Once we begin to focus on *getting* rather than on *giving* in a marital situation we engage in a type of behaviour that is self-defeating. Unconsciously we attempt to manipulate our partner to give us what we feel we need, and the energy we expend to accomplish this proves counter-productive, as it breaks the laws of relationships and works against the design of our loving Creator. Someone has said that 'love begins when it expects nothing in return'. Ask yourself now: Is this the kind of love I have in my heart for my partner? Can I be content to give without wanting something in return?

If you honestly answer 'No' to those questions don't be discouraged because, as I said, it is the central problem behind most marital difficulties. We mustn't leave things there, however, for we now have to move on to discover how we can become ministers rather than manipulators in our marriage.

A Christian husband must learn to look to Jesus Christ for the meeting of his need for significance, and a Christian wife similarly must look to the Lord for the meeting of her need for security. These personal needs can only genuinely and fully be met in a relationship with Jesus Christ. From the time we began life in this world each one of us attempted to meet our personal needs in self-centred ways. Ignoring God and His Son, Jesus Christ, we tried to find significance and security by following our own ideas and devices. Some of us might even have experienced a high degree of significance and security by these self-centred means, but it is impossible to find *true* significance or *true* security apart from a close and continuous relationship with Jesus Christ. We are *complete*, says the Apostle Paul, 'in Him' (Colossians 2.10). That is tantamount to saying – apart from Him we are incomplete, no matter how we might strive to meet our basic inner needs.

Let me now put this concept in the form of an illustration. A married woman I once counselled told me that she was feeling greatly unfulfilled in her marriage because her husband failed to notice the things she did for him and was irritatingly inattentive. In other words, she felt unloved, and because she felt unloved she was insecure. I explained to her that she didn't really need her husband's attention in order to feel secure as Christ had already made provision for the meeting of that need in her life by a relationship with Himself. At first she resisted the idea by saying no matter how real Christ was to her she still needed the loving attention of her husband in order to feel fulfilled. 'I am a human being,' she said, 'and I need to hear loving words, see affection in my husband's eyes, and feel his touch. God can't provide these visible things – except through my husband.' I told her that I sympathised with her feelings and understood how she longed for her husband's approval, but, nevertheless, her basic need, the need for security, could be met by Christ in such a way that although the longing for human approval would still be there, it would not present such a pressing problem. She agreed to meditate on a number of Scriptures I gave her, such as Colossians 2.10; Romans 8.35; Romans 5.8 and as a result of focussing on these passages she gradually came to see that in Christ she could find a sense of security that would help her face all of life's challenges with a different perspective. Her husband acted no differently toward her and proved the same inattentive person that he had been before, but inwardly *she* changed. Instead of manipulating her husband to try and get him to give her compliments, and approval, she began to focus on how she could best minister to him. At first her husband couldn't understand what was happening. She no longer nagged or scolded him, nor reproved or reprimanded him, so much so that the absence of this brought him to a deep spiritual crisis. He told me later 'the change in my wife forced me to examine my own inner attitudes and I came to realise I was not the man God wanted me to be.' That marriage began to function in a new way when the woman concerned found a position of strength in Christ, experienced a new touch of His power and from this position of strength began to minister to her husband. She became, as I said earlier, a giver rather than a getter, a minister not a manipulator, and functioned in her marriage from a position of strength rather than as before a position of weakness.

As we find true significance and security in Christ we are no longer under pressure to have our basic needs met, and thus we can be givers rather than getters. In giving God uses us to enrich the life of our partner.

Pictorially, the concepts I have dealt with would look like this:

GOD'S DESIGN

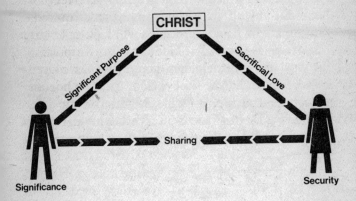

HUMAN MISUNDERSTANDING

There can be no greater thrill in marriage than the discovery that God selected you for the ministry of helping your partner understand his or her uniqueness and importance to God. As a first step toward substituting the joy of ministering to your partner, rather than manipulating him or her to meet your own needs, write out the following commitment and memorise it.

Although I enjoy any attention my partner may give me and I delight in getting my needs met, I commit myself to putting my partner's needs above my own and in future I will look upon my marriage as an opportunity to treat my spouse in a way that will help him/her realise how loved and valued he/she is by God. In dependency upon the Holy Spirit I will commit myself to this, believing that as I focus on meeting my partner's needs I will become a more fulfilled and satisfied person.

5

Live within your budget

A cartoon I saw some time ago depicted a newly-wed couple going on their honeymoon with a well-wisher saying 'Have a happy marriage'. The young bride replied 'Don't worry. We won't have any problems for we agree on most things – except money'. It reminded me of a story I heard about a couple getting married and when the bride was asked to repeat the phrase 'till death do us part' she slipped up and said instead 'Till *debt* do us part.' Unwittingly she added another exception to her marriage vows!

The Bible is full of exhortations, commands and warnings, about the subject of money. Greed is everywhere denounced in the Scriptures and generosity everywhere extolled. Someone has said that Jesus Christ had more to say about money and possessions than He did about both the subject of hell and heaven combined. Certainly almost every parable He spoke related in some way to money.

One of the major difficulties people run into in marriage is the problem of over spending. This is usually because there is no budget or detailed spending guide. Few people would begin a journey without a map. No builder would attempt to erect a building without a plan. Yet a recent survey indicated that only *one family in fourteen* used a simple family budget system.

A budget is simply a cash forecast – a list of upcoming expenditures over a given period of time. Every good business has one, and every Christian family concerned about the right use of the Lord's money should operate one. Remember, a budget is not necessarily a magic wand which you wave over your finances and hey presto, all your money problems disappear. It takes discipline to establish a budget and even more discipline to maintain it. How then does a family go about building a budget?

Establish your annual income and expenditure
Try to ascertain what you spent last year on all items. If you are unable to do this it may well be the reason for any financial difficulty you are experiencing. You might have over-spent because you failed to chart a proper course for your outgoings. The important thing is to know, as best you can, where your money goes. List your rent, mortgage repayments, insurances, telephone costs, food bills, car repayments, gas and electricity charges, etc. An unusual expense facing a family is often regarded by them as an 'emergency'. For example, if a £100 car insurance bill comes in during the month of March and there is no money to meet it, this can be a sudden blow to the finances. But the problem could have been largely overcome by proper budgeting. The budget would have foreseen the event and would have prepared for it by diverting a few

pounds a week into a special fund. This is why a budget is imperative – it helps forecast your expenditures *ahead of time*.

One of the greatest barriers to successful budgeting and money management is the ever present problem of credit. An investigation into the cause of family bankruptcies indicated that in almost every case the reason was over-use of credit. It is estimated that for every personal bankruptcy at least twenty other families are on the verge of it. Impatience to have luxuries of life too fast brings thousands into financial bondage. In a credit-oriented society a Christian should be alert to the use and abuse of the credit system. It should be seen as a convenience and nothing more. Credit facilities do have some advantages. Most of us use this facility from time to time when we buy electricity, gas, water, and the use of a telephone.

Another barrier to successful budgeting is that of high pressure advertising. Human nature, apart from the grace of God, is basically materialistic. We all have a tendency to want to live beyond our means. High pressure advertising however can pinch pounds out of your pocket. Advertisements such as these –'You owe it to yourself to take this fabulous holiday. Don't allow cash to be a handicap.' 'Fly now – Pay later' appeal to elements in our nature which if not carefully watched can lead us into serious financial difficulties. Advertisers (not all) aim at taking advantage of our psychological vulnerability and our carnal desires to line their own pockets.

Over the years I have counselled many people on the subject of finance. I am not an expert in this area by any means, but I know how easy it is to get trapped on a financial treadmill. Every day we are urged to live better . . . immediately . . . not later. Keeping up with the Joneses is no longer a joke: it is the very essense of modern day living. Even the most solemn and thrifty economists plead with us to part with our cash and use credit liberally. As Christians we ought to ask God to help us develop a *spiritual sales resistance* to such pleas so that we might become better stewards of the Lord's money which passes through our hands.

When couples come to me for pre-marital counselling they are usually surprised when I spend a good deal of time talking about their financial plans and budgeting. I encourage them to put themselves on a budget as soon as they enter married life. My own experience confirms what almost every Christian counsellor writes on the subject, namely that a most common cause of difficulty in marriage is disagreement over finances. So build a budget and stick with it. If you don't you will not live within your means and you will have continual conflict – regardless of how much money you have.

6

Establish clear guidelines for handling friction

Some years ago I met a man who said he and his wife had been married thirty years and in all their years of marriage they had only one argument. 'It started the day we were married' he said 'and to this moment it has not stopped!' Well, joking apart, every marriage has periods of argument, friction and conflict. Even the greatest saints in the Bible hit some difficult times in their marriages. Look at Abraham (Genesis 16), Isaac (Genesis 27), Jacob (Genesis 30, 31), Moses (Exodus 4), David (2 Samuel 6) and Hosea.

Conflicts are inevitable but they can, if you know how to handle them, improve your marriage rather than tear it apart. So decide right now that you will establish some clear guidelines for dealing with conflicts. The suggestions below are culled from many hours in counselling sessions helping Christians resolve their differences.

Firstly: determine to resolve every conflict rather than settling for peace at any price. A research conducted in the United States several years ago came up with the interesting information that there are five common styles of responding to conflict. We can *withdraw* from conflict by adopting the attitude 'Well I can't win so what's the use'. We can *set out to win* in a conflict and say to ourselves, 'If I don't win then I can't live with myself'. We can *yield* to conflict – give in in order to get along. We can *compromise* in a conflict; but the danger is we might compromise important principles. Finally we can *resolve* a conflict, by facing the root problem and getting to the bottom of the matter. This is the only way to approach conflict. All the other ways are 'cop-outs' because they don't make for a growing relationship. Growth and maturity develop when we face issues, not dodge them.

Secondly: deal with conflict issues as soon as possible after they occur. It is here that the man, being the leader of the home and the one responsible for the climate of love and freedom, must take the initiative for resolving the conflict, even if his wife 'has started the whole thing'. I realise that a man's feelings may be so deeply hurt by his wife's attitudes or actions that he may feel disinclined to take any initiative but at such times he should remind himself of the command of Jesus Christ in Ephesians 5: 'Husbands, love your wives as Christ loved the Church'. It may take a while for the truth of this scripture to sink through one's hurt and damaged emotions – but it must be faced. God not only raises the standard to unbelievable heights but He also provides the power by which we can reach up to it.

The man should say, 'Let's talk'. But be careful

not to follow the example of one young husband who, when trying to implement this principle, said to his wife, 'You've been acting like a two year old for the past few hours. Come here and let's talk.' He couldn't figure out why this made his wife angrier than before! The husband missed a vital point in the resolution of conflict and that is making 'I' statements rather than 'you' statements. 'You' statements are accusatory and put a person on the defensive. By saying 'You are acting like a two year old' the young husband brought the conversation to a shuddering halt even before it began. What he should have said is this 'I feel there is something wrong between us . . . please sit down and let's talk about it'.

Thirdly: Specifically define the problem or conflict issue. Here again the man taking the initiative should say, 'As I understand it the problem appears to be . . .' then indicate the problem. Be careful, however, to simply state the problem and not be defensive. It would be inappropriate, for example, to say 'As I understand the problem you are getting unnecessarily upset with me over the fact that I came home late from work'. The word 'unnecessarily' here is a defensive word and adds to the problem at this stage. Simply keep to the facts and avoid any emotive words or language.

Make sure that the problem or issue is defined so that you both know what it is you need to talk about and that both of you understand it.

Fourthly: Focus on the problem and not on each other. If a problem arises because the husband arrives home late, upsetting the domestic routine, then this should be the subject for discussion. It is impossible, of course, in the heat of an argument for a subject to be discussed academically, as feelings have been aroused and possibly hurt, but, as far as possible, each partner should focus on the problem and not so much on the person. Feelings *have* to be aired and it is here that the admonition of Paul, speaking the truth in love (Ephesians 4.15) must be the watchword. Couples should commit themselves, long before any arguments arise, to speaking the truth in love on all occasions. Without this commitment there can be little hope of resolving differences. How therefore do you air your feelings without venting them on your partner? You do it by accepting responsibility for the way you feel. Never say, for example, 'You make me so angry' because no one can really *make* you angry – you *become* angry because you respond wrongly to a situation. What you should say is 'I feel angry' or 'I am feeling deeply hurt'. This shows your partner that you are feeling hurt but doesn't imply blame.

Fifthly: Make up your mind to end every conflict by seeking forgiveness or being the one to forgive. This is the most important part of conflict resolution. It determines whether you are merely lowering the heat or turning it off completely. It takes two to tango, as the saying goes, and if you are a participant in a shouting match then you are part of the problem. Perhaps your partner did *start* it and began shouting at you, but if you shouted back then you have a responsibility in the matter, too. And even if you were just one per cent wrong, and your partner was ninety-nine per cent wrong, then you still need to ask forgiveness for your one per cent. Asking forgiveness is one of the most humbling yet most gratifying acts you can perform for your marriage. Remember, time does not heal wounds – only forgiveness can do that. For without forgiveness time will simply give the hurt more opportunity to grow roots.

Together, ahead of time, draw up a set of rules for handling conflict. Then when the conflict arises talk about it. Listen to each other and abide by the rules. Be quick to apologise or ask for forgiveness. Ephesians 4.32 is a favourite verse of mine and I use it in my own marriage as well as when I am counselling couples: 'Be kind to one another, tender-hearted, forgiving one another as God, for Christ's sake, has forgiven you'. Focussing on how much God has forgiven you produces the grace to forgive one another. You do it – for Christ's sake.

7

Cultivate a good sexual relationship

It is surprising how many Christian couples have hang-ups over the subject of sex. There are still some people who think that sex in marriage is something you do when God is not looking! God creates us as sexual beings as is evident from the statement 'Male and female created he them' (Genesis 5.2). Isn't it interesting that in the first statement God made about His human creation He underlined the fact that they were biologically (and psychologically) different? The gift of sexuality has provided man and woman, within the marriage bond, with the most complete way to express and share the love God intends them to have with each other.

The Christian Church over the centuries has suffered from many un-Scriptural conclusions about the subject of sex. Clement of Alexandria said 'marriage is sacred: it must be kept free from physical contact.' Origen, another of the Church's Fathers, said 'Adam did not have sexual knowledge of his wife until after the fall. If it wasn't for the fall the human race would probably have been propogated in some mysterious or angelic manner without sex, and therefore without sin.' During the middle ages some theologians believed that the Holy Spirit left the room when two married people had intercourse, even though it were for the purpose of conceiving a child. We have inherited many false notions about sex from the past and we Christians must get back to the Bible and see what the Scriptures have to say on the subject.

We have already observed that sex and marriage are of Divine origin in these words, 'Male and female created he them.' Here are a few more Scriptures as a basis for coming to some sound conclusions about the subject of sex.

– Human sexuality carries God's unqualified approval: 'And God saw *everything* he had made and behold it was very good'. Genesis 1.31.

– Sex and marriage were God's gift prior to the fall: 'And God blessed them and God said unto them, Be fruitful and multiply'. Genesis 1.27.

– Sex exists not *only* for the purposes of procreation. It is the means by which married partners can give physical pleasure to each other, as can be seen from an examination of such Scriptures as the Song of Solomon, Proverbs 5.15–21, Deut. 24.5.

When counselling couples on the subject of sex I give them the following advice –

Educate yourself in basic sexual matters: Every man and woman should have a basic knowledge of the male and female anatomy. The Biblical statement 'My people are destroyed for lack of knowledge' (Hosea 4.6) is as true in matters of sexual understanding as it is in matters of spiritual truth. Today you can buy hundreds of books on the subject of sex and marriage. Some are educational and some set out to be erotic. Visit a Christian bookshop and ask advice on the subject. Any steps you take to educate yourself in relation to the basic facts of sexual performance will most certainly pay off in your relationship.

Be alert to the psychological differences between the male and female personality: I have found that one of the major problems between married couples in relation to the matter of sex is because they fail to recognise the important psychological differences between a man and a woman. A man, for example, is aroused sexually by what he *sees*: a woman is stimulated more by what she *hears*. When a man watches his wife undress in preparation for going to bed he often becomes ready to engage in sexual intercourse. He sometimes forgets, however, that his wife does not respond as readily to the idea of sex as he does and then fails to be as understanding and tender as he ought in seeking to bring her to sexual readiness. To a woman sex begins not in the bedroom but in the living room. She sees sex as beginning in a tender touch, continuing with affectionate words, and then some time later reaching its climax in the act of intercourse. One woman I know told her husband in a counselling session, 'I wish you would act lovingly to me as soon as you come home at night, then perhaps I'd be ready for passion and intimacy by bedtime'.

Keep in mind that a husband and wife are responsible to meet each other's sexual needs all of their lives. Paul put it this way: 'The man should give his wife all that is her right as a married woman, and the wife should do the same for her husband . . . . So do not refuse these rights to each other.' (1 Corinthians 7.3–5 TLB). The husband is responsible to meet his wife's sexual needs. He must lovingly and tenderly arouse her to as complete sexual experience as possible. Likewise, the wife must meet her husband's sexual needs. She must regularly and lovingly arouse him to as complete sexual experience as possible. A husband should not expect his wife to meet her sexual needs through masturbation and neither should a wife expect her husband to meet his own sexual needs in this way. If they are motivated by love they will want to meet each other's sexual needs, for as I have said before, it is only through giving that we truly receive. In the Scripture I quoted above, Paul goes on to say 'For the wife does not rule over her own body, but the husband does; likewise the husband does not rule over his own body, but the wife does.' In marriage the wife's body does not belong to her, but to her husband – and he rules over it. In like manner the husband's body does not belong to him but to his wife and she rules over it. This concept needs to be in the forefront of every married couple's thinking for it is then it breaks the vicious circle of self centredness and motivates a man and a woman to be givers and not takers in the relationship.

8

Extend common courtesies towards each other

Courtesy and manners are a grace that should be part of every Christian's life, but in this modern generation they seem to be a dying art. A minister tells of how he announced one evening to the men in his church that the next week he would speak on the subject: 'How to get your wife to treat you like a king.' When the night came on which he was to address the men's group he discovered that long before the service was due to start every seat was filled. Somehow the word had got around to all the men in his church constituency that this was to be the subject and the result was a packed church. Some were quite startled by the simplicity of his formula for 'getting your wife to treat you like a king'. It was this – 'Treat her like a queen'.

A similar formula could be adopted for wives who would like their husbands to treat them like a queen – treat him like a king. Be thoughtful to each other for it is the little things that help to build a good and lasting relationship. Husbands, open the door for your wife. Wives, say respectful and encouraging things to your husband. Both of you should be as polite to one another inside the home as you are are when you are out.

Never air your partner's shortcomings, weaknesses, or deficiencies in front of other people. Never criticise your partner to friends or relatives. If you have anything to say which expresses displeasure then share it with your partner only – never with anyone else. You should never criticise your partner to others, for two special reasons. One, the more you rehearse your grudges or gripes the more indelibly impressed they will become in your mind. Two, nothing causes a person to feel 'let down' more than knowing that their partner has been disloyal to them by criticising them to someone else.

Husbands, if you are finding the excitement beginning to disappear from your marriage here is a way you can make it re-appear. Buy your wife a box of chocolates, or some other inexpensive but well chosen gift, and as you give it to her explain that you just wanted to show her a little token of your affection and appreciation for the pleasure she gives you in your marriage. Always remember that a woman appreciates the small and unexpected gifts more than she does the ones dutifully presented to her on her birthday or wedding anniversary.

Wives, you can best bring pleasure to your husbands by endeavouring to look as well groomed as possible. Appearance isn't everything but when a woman takes time and trouble to be neat and clean in her appearance, particularly when her husband comes home from work, this brings him a tremendous sense of pleasure. Take a few minutes before your husband returns home to put on a clean dress, comb your hair and, if you can, meet him at the front door, looking as if you had just stepped out of a band box. He might faint at your first attempt, but as you maintain this courtesy, it will help you recapture the same romantic atmosphere you enjoyed during your courtship days.

Common courtesy and minding your manners refers to such simple things also as cleanliness of body, speech and clothing. It means respect and thoughtfulness. It is a husband remembering to telephone his wife if he sees he is going to be late home. It is a wife slipping a note into her husband's meal-pack to say 'I love you'. It is a man walking side by side with his wife instead of three or four paces ahead of her. It is a woman refraining from loading on to her husband the difficulties of her day until he has eaten his evening meal.

Another important thing is to discover the sensitive area in your partner's life. Husbands, find out what it is about you that most irritates your wife. Wives, find out what it is about you that most bothers your husband. It's more than likely you have no idea what about you is most offensive to your partner. Several years ago, after returning from a family conference where someone suggested this idea to me, I asked my wife what habit or behaviour pattern in my life offended her. I thought I knew what her answer would be. In fact there were several things I expected her to mention but the one thing she pinpointed was something I thought did not bother her at all. So much for my sensitivity!

We then turned the situation around and a similar thing happened. I mentioned something about her that I found irritating which she was completely unaware of. We both began to work on these irritations immediately and I'm glad to say that within a matter of months we found they had disappeared from our individual lifestyle.

Husbands, take your wife out on a date once a week, or at least once a month. It doesn't have to be an expensive restaurant, but most certainly choose one that is not overcrowded. When I suggested this to a man some time ago, he told me, 'I have not taken my wife out for close on six months. I'll telephone her now and arrange to take her out tonight.' He thereupon phoned her and made the appointment. I saw him several weeks later and asked him how he had got on. He replied 'It was a disaster.' Seeing my expression of surprise he hastened to explain. 'Halfway through dinner' he said 'my wife turned to me and said "Tom, I can't tell you how much this evening means to me. I want you to know that I appreciate this more than words can convey." ' Tom replied, 'Yes, Selwyn said it would be a good idea to do this; I'm glad to see it worked.' Needless to say it ruined the whole evening!

Another courtesy married couples should employ is that of keeping no secrets from each other. Honestly share your fears, your hopes, and your dreams. Someone said 'Marriage is one of the chief ways God has of explaining Himself.' Think of it! Daily in our marriages we can find out something about God and display something of Christ's love for His Church through each other. Small wonder then that the chief thing Satan seeks to vandalise is the demonstrated love and closeness between married couples. Resist, as you would a plague, any tendency within you toward taking your partner for granted.

9

Seek to become emotionally mature

A dictionary definition of maturity is 'full development of mind, body and spirit.' Most of us, I am sure, will fail to qualify on that count. We all have, to a greater or lesser degree, immature spots in our make-up. Someone has said that 'in the area of emotional maturity a person has to be able to rely on himself, take responsibility for his own actions, know that what happens to him is not half as important as what he does about it, and learns from every experience he undergoes.' David Mace, described by someone as the 'dean of marriage guidance counsellors', said 'There are no unhappy marriages – only marriage partners who are immature.'

Many people go into marriage hoping that in some way it will help them overcome their emotional immaturity. But marriage, in itself, doesn't solve our emotional problems. It merely gives them a new arena in which to work. An emotionally immature person is not suddenly made mature upon entering marriage. Those magic words spoken at the altar do not suddenly make you grow up emotionally. One of life's tragedies is the fact that people grow up physically and reach the age when they can legally be married but they never grow up in their emotions. Such a person is still a child whose life is characterised by sheer childishness, selfishness, temper tantrums, or I-want-what-I-want-when-I-want-it attitudes. This is why it is often said, you are not really ready to be happily married to another person until you are happily married to yourself.

Whenever I am approached to counsel a broken marriage I find, upon examination, that almost without exception a basic problem is that of immature attitudes and immature behaviour. Hugh Missildine in his famous book *Your Inner Child of the Past* says that 'Somewhere, sometime you were a child. Yet the fact that you were once a child has an important bearing on your life today. Your childhood in actual literal sense exists within you now. It not only continues to survive, but in some cases to *thrive*. Often this inner child of the past dominates your life, your attitudes, your behaviour, your ideas, your concepts, even now you are an adult.' Unless we learn to do as the Apostle Paul tells us, that is, 'put away childish things' then these childish attitudes will intrude into our adult behaviour and produce serious disturbances in our relationships, particularly in marriage.

The following family scene will help to illustrate what I am saying.

David was late again for dinner. 'Where have you been until now?' demanded his wife, Elaine, as he entered the house. 'I've kept the dinner waiting for two hours. Everything is ruined. Couldn't you have got a message to me?' David's response was to go into a temper tantrum. 'There you go again' he said to Elaine, 'trying to run my life. If you think I'm going to get a message to you whenever I am late then you will have to think again. Who do you think you are expecting me to give an account of myself for everything I do. I'll come home just when I please. I earn the money. I pay the bills. I don't have to give account of myself to you.' 'But David' said Elaine 'I'm not asking you to give account of yourself. I'm just asking you to come home to dinner on time. The children and I want to sit down with you at dinner time. Don't you care about that?' 'There you go again' said David, 'using the children to try and force me to be obedient.' When I counselled David it appeared to be a surprise to him to learn that his wife really did love him and was not trying to force him to be obedient to her. He found, in fact, that the real problem was his inner child of the past. When he was a child his mother seldom gave him definite instructions about anything and whenever he was punished he had only the vaguest idea as to why he was being disciplined. David's mother left him with a feeling of being guilty and that, try as he would, he could never please her – no matter what he did. Consequently, David never outgrew those emotional deprivations, and whenever his wife objected to his behaviour he was unable to perceive that his reactions were based on the problem of his past.

In counselling, David discovered that he was really

stumbling over the shadow of his mother's influence and that his wife's requests were not insistent demands but expressions of concern. He came to see that his inner child of the past was acting up and that now, as a man, he must decide to act and not to re-act. In other words, to determine in his heart not to be pushed around by the immaturities of his past but to grow up and face life with a more mature outlook. Casting off these infantile complexes is not easy and if you find any difficulty in this area don't hesitate to talk to a minister or an experienced Christian counsellor.

The Christian Church, I believe, has missed its way here in relation to this matter of emotional maturity. It is one of the most neglected areas of Christian thought and teaching. Some of the greatest marital problems arise in this area causing the break-up of the finest Christian marriages. Spiritual maturity and emotional maturity are integrated. If a person continues to function at an immature level where his inner child of the past is in control of his emotions then his spiritual maturity will remain on the same level. It is only when the emotional level is dealt with that a person has the freedom to grow spiritually.

Many have come into the Chritian Church and been taught that the solution to every problem is a directly spiritual one. In such circles anyone complaining of emotional difficulties is told, 'Read your Bible and pray more.' Now there is no one with a higher view of the Scriptures than I and no one who believes more in prayer than I do, but there are problems which need a little more practical advice, especially those that have to do with hurt or damaged emotions. Believe me, I have known some extremely unhappy Christian couples struggle along for years unable to change neurotic patterns in their marriages because they were told that their problems were 'spiritual' and would respond only to more Bible reading, more church attendance and more personal prayer.

One of the basic traits of a mature person is being able to control his emotions whatever they may be, and not let the emotions control him. If you have problems in this area then begin by deciding to do what the Apostle Paul advises in 1 Corinthians 13.11. 'When I was a child I spoke as a child, I understood as a child, I thought as a child, but when I became a man I put away childish things.' The English words 'put away' in this text come from a Greek work *katageo* which means to disconnect or render inoperative. You move toward greater maturity in your emotional life when you *make up your mind* to stop acting childishly and deal with life's issues on a more adult level.

10

Share together in daily Bible reading and prayer

We cannot finish our theme of *Happiness in Marriage* without reference to the importance of Scripture reading and prayer. Some Christians call the procedure of reading the Scriptures and praying together the 'Family Altar'. A family altar is not a mysterious or ethereal experience, but a simple matter of reading the Bible and praying together at a definite time each day. Here are a few suggestions on how to establish a Family Altar.

– Decide upon a time, either morning or evening, when you meet together for Bible reading and prayer. Keep to this faithfully unless, of course, an emergency occurs that necessitates adjustment. Whenever I counsel engaged couples, or those about to be married, I advise them to begin this on their wedding night. But remember, it's never too late to start one.

– Read a passage from the Scriptures, and discuss some aspect of the reading which interests you. Some couples like to read a chapter a day while others prefer a short passage. Across the British Isles and in other parts of the world thousands of people follow the daily devotional I write, entitled *Every Day with Jesus*. This publication is designed to assist one's devotional life by pursuing a Biblical theme over a period of two months and looks at different passages of Scripture each day as they relate to the general theme. There are many other devotional and Bible study aids, and a visit to your local Christian bookshop will soon acquaint you with these.

– Prayer should then be made by both husband and wife. You may wish, of course, to have your own personal time of prayer at some other point in the day, but in order to grow together spiritually it is necessary to pray together. I have found that the majority of Christian couples are embarrassed to pray together. The reasons for this must be carefully examined and overcome, for the corporate prayer life of couples provides a stability that is refreshing, enjoyable and helpful to the ongoing health of the marriage. Listen to what the Scripture says about the power of praying together: 'Again, I tell you, if two of you on earth agree (harmonise together, make a symphony) about anything and everything whatever they shall ask, it will come to pass and be done for them by my Father in heaven. For wherever two or three are gathered (drawn together as My followers) in (into) My Name there I AM in the midst of them' (Matthew 18.19 Amplified New Testament).

One of the most helpful suggestions regarding prayer in the marriage relationship I have heard comes from Dr Tim LaHaye of San Diego,

California. This is how it works: each time the couple meet together one of the partners leads in prayer by praying for the issue closest to heart. The other partner then follows, praying also for the same thing. The one who initiated the prayer session then prays over the next burden on his or her heart, and the other partner takes this up and continues praying for the same thing. This procedure continues until they have completed their allotted prayer time.

The next day the procedure is reversed. The one who in the previous meeting followed in prayer, now leads, the other partner taking up the burden and continuing to uphold the issue in prayer. This approach to prayer helps to develop a spiritual and psychological oneness in the life of a married couple, for as they share each other's burdens there develops between them a closeness that is truly remarkable. Such sharing deepens the common bond that exists between a man and his wife and contributes greatly to the happiness of a marriage.

When a married couple engage in daily reading of the Scriptures combined with prayer and worship, the experience makes a great impact upon their lives. One cannot go through such a daily encounter without feeling its effects. One cannot pray without perspectives being changed. God's Word cannot be opened without results taking place. There are many glowing stories of couples who have introduced a Family Altar into their marriage to find that it transformed their relationship and deepened their lives in the most amazing way. You can expect maximum results from a Family Altar. It is the biggest single contribution to a happy and successful marriage.

A marriage check-up

Remember your marriage vows? 'For better . . . for worse . . . in sickness . . . and in health . . . to love and to cherish . . .' A wedding anniversary is a good time to talk over your marriage, and to consider how well things are working out. We go for check-ups with our dentist or doctor, so that through wise, preventative, measures we can ensure good physical health. An occasional marriage check-up, taken seriously, prayerfully and intelligently, will help to maintain good emotional health in our marriage.

Here are some questions which a husband and wife might discuss together. If there is a problem, discussion will help to clarify it, and can, sometimes, invigorate the whole atmosphere of a marriage.

1. Communication
   1. Do we have enough time for quiet talks together?
   2. How much do we listen to each other, and hear exactly what is being said?
   3. How often do we make the mistake of

attacking each other's personality rather than the problem?

4. How can we build a better communication system between us than we have at present?

2. Love

A Christian has a tremendous advantage over a non Christian, inasmuch as he or she has access to a flow of Divine Love, which enables them to love to a much deeper degree. Divine Love delights more in giving than in receiving.

1. In what ways do we honestly try to please each other?

2. Have we yet reached that 'sacrificial love' of which the Scripture speaks, in which we delight more to be a giver than a receiver?

3. In what ways do we show we are truly concerned for each others hurts?

4. How can we develop an even greater love for each other?

3. Finances

1. Are we happy with the way we are managing our finances?

2. Does God have His share in our weekly or monthly outgoings?

3. Are we living within a properly constructed budget?

4. What can we do to improve the handling of our finances?

4. Temperament

1. Do we recognise that God has designed us with different temperaments?

2. Are we trying to change each other, rather

than improve ourselves?

3. Are we mature enough to realise that marriage needs constant adjustment and compromise where temperament is concerned?

4. Are we miserly with our criticism and lavish with our praise?

5. Sex

1. Does sexual intercourse bring us pleasure and a feeling of unity and fulfilment?

2. Are we concerned, when love-making, merely in getting something for ourselves, rather than giving to the other?

3. To what extent are we aware of each other's individual variations and differences regarding sexual needs?

4. Have we learned to distinguish the difference between lust and love? (Lust can never wait to get: Love can always wait to give)

6. In-laws

1. Is there any resentment, or bitterness, against our father-in-law or mother-in-law?

2. Do we maintain a happy and meaningful relationship with them?

3. Can we listen to what they say without being over-influenced by their remarks?

4. Are there ways in which we can help them without compromising our necessary independence?

7. Recreation and social activities

1. Are we happy about the ways in which we seek to relax?

2. Are our social activities causing us to spend

more time with friends than with each other?

3. Do we plan our holidays well ahead?
4. Do we respect each other's likes and dislikes in relation to the matter of recreation?

8. Spiritual
   1. Do we spend enough time together in prayer?
   2. Is the Bible reading and church attendance what it should be?
   3. Are we open and honest with each other in everything, maintaining a clean and clear conscience on all matters?
   4. Is there anything more that we can do to improve our spiritual relationship with the Lord and with each other?

9. Children
   1. Are we presenting a good parental image to our children?
   2. Do we discipline them effectively, or are we guilty of under-discipline, over-discipline or don't discipline at all?
   3. Do we make sure that we have time for them and make them feel loved?
   4. In what way can we be better parents?

10. Our emerging family pattern
    1. Have we clarified and accepted our respective roles as husband and wife?
    2. What definite family goals are we working toward?
    3. Do we remember birthdays, anniversaries and special occasions?

4. What more could we do to contribute to the success of our family relationships?

On this special day, dedicate yourself afresh to God and to each other. If you need further counselling or help, contact us at The Christian Counselling Centre.

Epilogue

Firstly, likewise you wives, be submissive to your husbands . . .
Let not yours be the outward adorning with braiding of hair, decoration of gold, and wearing of robes, but

Let it be in the inner person of the heart with the imperishable jewel of a gentle hand and quiet spirit, which in God's sight is very precious . . .

Likewise you husbands, live considerately with your wives,

Bestowing honour on the woman as the weaker sex,

Since you are joint heirs of the grace of life, in order that your prayers may not be hindered.

Finally, to both of you, have unity of spirit, sympathy, love of the brethren, a tender heart and a humble mind . . .
Bless, for to this you have been called, that you may obtain a blessing.

For he that would love life and see good days . . .
let him turn away from evil and do right.
Let him seek peace and pursue it.

For the eyes of the Lord are upon the righteous,
and his ears are open to their prayer.

1 Peter 3.1–12.